"LIFE AFTER LIFE"

The Untold Stories Of Life In And Out
Of My Season Of Incarceration

authorHOUSE®

AuthorHouse™
1663 Liberty Drive
Bloomington, IN 47403
www.authorhouse.com
Phone: 1 (800) 839-8640

Published by AuthorHouse 01/17/2018

ISBN: 978-1-5462-1448-9 (sc)
ISBN: 978-1-5462-1447-2 (e)

Library of Congress Control Number: 2017916515

Print information available on the last page.

CONTENTS

Encouraging Poems

PREFACE

Father I ask that you bless the reader of this book. I ask that you release the comfort of your presence and Holy Spirit upon each one so that they may experience your sincerity. Through the humility of your willing servant, write and impart the triumphs, adversities, and trials of afflictions. Share all of the broken pieces that you have taken upon your love and put them back together. Make a testimony and let it be a reflection unto them, that all brokenness', whatever they are, can be put back together if it is returned to The Potter's hand. Make it so that it will be used for your will.

-Amen

AKNOWLEDGEMENT

I truly thank God first. He has allowed me another opportunity to write, share, and express the many encounters I have had in both my life and my life incarcerated. I give all glory to Him, for it would not be possible to have lived my life without the tremendous amount of mercy and grace that He has given unto me through the sacrifice and love of His son Jesus Christ. Honestly there is no other way I can or need to put it. There is no other reason that I am breathing today. There is no other reason that I am free today. For that, I choose to give honor where and to whom it belongs. I will not place anyone or anything else upon this page because it is by Him that I present unto you "LIFE AFTER LIFE": The Untold Stories.

Thank You Lord JESUS!

CHAPTER 1

"The Day I Sat Down With The Philistine Giant And Shared The Book Of Life"

There are many things I would have desired first to do, but of the many, I choose to write and share this with you.

Life…what is the meaning?

I know we all could come up with many definitions on such a topic but at this point, I would like to share a story of life with you, not only my life but life after life. You see it all starts with the very first steps that I took June 10th, 2010 as a free man. These first steps were after many steps while in incarceration from serving a natural life sentence.

You, the reader, will truly have to take a seat for this is a remarkable telltale story of an 18-year journey from a natural life sentence to a life of freedom.

In this life of freedom, I get to choose to go where I want, eat what I want, visit who I want, shower as long as I want, run as far as I want, stay up as long as I want, and even get up as late as I want. "Wow" was the word that was upon my lips and every other word after that was mingled with "Wow" when I first journeyed into the world as a free man. Oh, how things had changed over the course of 18 years. I was in a state of amazement because of how different everything and everyone looked. Cars looked futuristic and it was literally as if I had stepped out of the movie that I had enjoyed watching growing up as a kid "Back to the Future". This time however it wasn't a movie, it was my reality. From that point on there were times of overwhelming joy that I could not contain. I had moments that caused me to shout "Thank you" to the Heavens and there were moments where I cried tears of joy. My mind was trying to catch up with my reality because it was as if it was only yesterday that I recalled the memory of my upcoming days of my release. The day I would come to call "The Day I Sat Down with the Philistine Giant".

While incarcerated, each morning before they would call breakfast I would go to the dayroom while it was still early and read the Bible. See in prison if you don't get up early to eat then you won't eat at all. I utilized this time to rise early and seek the Lord. I must be honest, if I had not sought Him I would not be here today writing this story of my testimony. Most mornings I would be there while others were going to breakfast and from time to time there would be an inmate who would come by to sit and ask questions about the Bible or my Faith. I knew that many were hungry for the Lord but were not yet willing to sit down and Sup with Him. There were many being drawn to Him out of curiosity instead of a drawing expectation of encountering Him. I usually enjoyed spending time sitting and sharing my faith with them. I would answer any questions that they may have had but I made sure to never get into a debate over the Gospel; it was always a casual conversation. I always held close to the impression that the Lord had imparted on me; "I did not call on you to prove the Gospel but to preach the Gospel for it is self-proven". On this one particular morning, "The Day I Sat Down with the Philistine Giant", I was sitting at the table I usually sat at to read my Bible. It was sort of my multi-purpose table because at times I would read my Bible there and other times I would play chess or a nice of game of spades. Everything was going on, as usual, that morning and everyone was headed out to breakfast. I had just sat down, laid open my bible, and bowed my head to pray. As I lifted my head from praying, to my amazement, there was an inmate sitting at the table with me. The reason for my surprise was because this was not just any ordinary inmate. As I sat there with my eyes a little larger than usual gazing at the inmate that had just sat down I found myself a little discomforted by his presence. His stature was huge, not only in size but also the bulk of his arms. It was as if they were replaced with a second set of his legs. Although he was a huge muscular powerhouse his reputation far exceeded his stature. It was well known that no other inmates wanted to be around him due to the very violent and gruesome crimes he had committed. He was in for multiple murders in various heinous ways and he was also known for having killed other inmates while incarcerated. Even though the other inmates avoided him on purpose they also respected him enough to just avoid having contact with him. No one dared to bunk with him because one of the men that he killed in prison was his Bunkie and the rumor was that they had a disagreement and he waited until the other man went to sleep and took his TV and smashed his face in. So, to say the least, he had quite the reputation as someone to be watched and feared. Well here he was sitting at my table and I was quite alarmed to lift up my head from prayer only to find him sitting there. So as I took a deep breath I began to wonder if I should say something or not because in the back of my mind were all of the rumors and dreadful prison stories that many other inmates and guards had shared. I couldn't decide what to do so I begin to bow my head again to try and

focus on reading my Bible when suddenly he said: "Man,
I have been watching you." At first, I did not know how
to take such a statement because let us not forget that I
am in prison and the first rule of thumb that any inmate
is taught is "Do not drop the soap." Second, when another
man tells you that he has been watching you and you are
both in prison, every flag and antenna goes up, and pride
begins to go into defense mode. On the other hand, I
did have my faith and trust in the Lord for I was in my
18th year of incarceration and the Lord had kept me and
protected me numerous times of which anything could
have happened in a moment's notice without any warning.
I lifted up my head in a calm manner and looked him
right in the face and said with a right firm tone "Excuse
Me!" He then repeated the same words "Man I have been
watching you. You're always here at the same time every
morning. You sit at this table and I notice from time to
time that others come and sit at the table with you. You
begin to talk with them and read to them and sometimes,
from what it looks like, you pray for them." Now honestly
this was the farthest thing from my mind and I had not
prepared for him to say anything like that. My defense
mode quickly shifted because I now understood what he
meant when he said: "Man I have been watching you."
His statement was no longer coming across as aggressive
but more curiosity for something far deeper than what
was being seen on the surface. Something had caused a
deeper yearning in him that he could no longer ignore.
When this occurs I often wonder how many others may
be just like James, riddled with haunting convictions or

may even have a taunting past reputation and yet are hungering for change. What if they are only waiting to see that change in someone that is different than the norm? You see what I learned that day as I sat there with him and as I would with any other inmate that would stop by and get a word of hope or encouragement or at many times just a word of prayer. James and I had deep conversations and he was always asking if I believed he could or would be forgiven. You see I do not want to go into much detail but he had committed some very gruesome murders, and he suffered from a great deal of anger and resentment as a result. After some time, I soon came to realize he had cast a sense of unwillingness to feel anything close to empathy. After he had done so much and from the way all others had viewed him he had lived in this state of heartlessness and he felt that all sense of hope was gone. In his mind, he had nothing else to lose either so he kept up that shield of hopelessness to somewhat cover him so he would not have to face the reality of how much he had done. Yet it still could not root out the curiosity of him finding the courage to step out what was the norm for him and to sit at a table with a man that he had been watching read his Bible and pray with others. After some time he began to share some of the very gruesome stories of what he had done.

Now I am about to share a very moving moment from my last conversation with James, or shall I say it had to be the Lord in control of my lips.

Other inmates from time to time would come into the Dayroom and find James sitting at my table and they sit near and watch with amazement. Reason one, the man was known to just snap in a second and anything could set him off. He could seem normal and in all of a second would snap. As I described earlier, he was two or three sizes bigger than me and the man's arms looked like legs. He would've had no problem with getting a hold of a neck and snapping it in two. At the time that this occurred, I had only seven days left before I was to be released. I had already finished up my Physic Evaluation, my medical records, and the Governors Pardon had already been signed. I was still making my daily morning visits to my table which I have come now to know was my Alter.

I encourage you or anyone that is reading this book to find a place that you can take some time out of your day and commune, fellowship, read your Bible, or pray. In other words, you don't have to wait until you get to a place where you only congregate once a week make your an Alter. Your Alter should be somewhere you can go every day of the week to spend time with your Lord. This place should be one that you can use to give light to someone's darkness or become a simple drink for the one that may be have a thirst for righteousness.

On the 7th day before my release James was sitting at the table and it was as if I could not hold it in any longer because there was a part of me sensing that James still had a bit of his past reputation holding him back from truly being free and experiencing a righteous brokenness that only Jesus righteousness could bring. You see I had sensed that James had no fear of God due to all of the killing and wrong he has done. So many other men feared him, even other men that had killed before but it was like he had no fear of anything or anyone and because of that James had no fear of God. It was at that moment, seven days before my release that I believe the Lord took control of my lips. There is no explanation other than God, for the following words that came from my mouth on that day.

James came in and sat once again at my table and without any warning, I said "James, look at me." he then stared at me in a state of confusion, because the tone of my voice was a little firm and somewhat with authority. I then said, "You are not ready to see the Devil on his terms" and with a face of confusion he looked and said "What?" I then begin to tell him that if God was to show him, we must zip off this flesh and when we are able to see into the spirit realm that he would see that he was not ready to meet the Devil on his terms. I did not care how many lives he took or how many people there was that feared him, I told James that the moment we must see Him it cannot be on his terms. I shared with Him that the Devil is not moved by fear for He is fear. No human was made or is prepared to see Him on His terms other than the one who had defeated him with perfect love which cast out all fear and that was the one and only Jesus Christ.

James then began to get agitated. I could tell as his eyes squinted and his fist began to clutch one to another. I could tell he was not ready for what had just come out of my mouth and neither was I for that matter. The Lord has his way and surely I must say he was having it for the both of us at this moment. I went on and begin to share that he has no idea all of the fearful things that the devil desires to fulfill through him. I told him that up to this point he had been arm in arm with the devil and that the devil was using him to strike fear in others and carry out such heinous acts. I said to him "This small grace period that the Lord has allowed for you to be untormented and come sit with a man is because you have been watching him read his Bible and at other times pray. James, the Lord Jesus has already paid a price that you and I could not pay and has died a death, which he did not deserve, for you and me." After sharing many other things that the Lord had placed on my heart, James looked up with his eyes full of tears and began to sob. To my amazement and other inmates that were at other tables playing Chess or Cards looked with hesitation and looked as if to ask what the heck is going on. Some knew that we would be there from time to time talking or me just sharing a few words of encouragement. What they didn't know, however, was the extent of my conversations with this man in which many feared and would have no dealings with. They had no idea why he was sitting there crying instead of tearing up the dayroom. That is why I now come to call this moment "The Day That The Lord Had Me Sit Down with the Philistine Giant".

I remember the day of my release so clearly. The guard called my name on the mic system "235904" and as I walked out of my cell I noticed that all of the other inmates had formed a line from my cell door down the stairs to the door that leaves the unit. As I walked down the stairs, shaking hands and giving hugs, there were not only tears in their eyes but also in mine. There was a face in the crowd that outshined the others and that was James's. We shared our tears and a hug before his goodbye. He said "Thank you." and I then asked him "For what?" he then leaned and said "For all the lives I took, God has allowed me to see I am not prepared to see the Devil on His Terms. I must change my life."

"There Is no need to slay every Philistine Giant for with grace abound one simply has to take the time to share the Book of Life"

CHAPTER 2

"Just Another Day At The Office, or So I Thought"

Well it was a usual typical Monday I had to be on my Detail which interprets in "Prison Language" means a job. You do not get to choose what department the detail is in so when my Classification Coordinator told me that he had a detail for me I agreed immediately before even hearing which department it was for. To my amazement, I landed in Health Services as a Hospital Porter which happened to be the most sought-after department in which so many other inmates wanted this detail, not for the right reason of course. Their reasons were nurses and being in their current place of residency that is why so many inmates had put in for this sort of work detail. Other inmates were jealous and were questioning me about how I got the Healthcare work detail. Looking back now, with me being new, I really shouldn't have gotten it. Their questioning went on for quite some time but eventually, it died down. It ended up being a great detail because it got me out of my cell and there were a lot of perks that came along with it. My job description was to keep the healthcare area clean as well as buffing and waxing the floors. I literally loved my detail because I had a small mop closet that the guards and healthcare staff gave me which I turned it into a porter closet. It was a place that I could go from time to time to just get some peace. It was my little haven. I enjoyed going to work because it meant that I could go into my own little quiet space and just have me some quiet time but I did not know all of that would come to a screaming halt shortly.

It was another typical Monday so I thought. I had just begun cleaning the waiting area where inmates sit and wait for the doctor or nurse to see them. The waiting area pretty much stayed full that day seeing as though that there are no healthcare calls made on the weekend so Monday's are usually busy. I was in the swing of things and had just gone to my office/mop closet to get the dust mop so that I could start making my way toward the inmate waiting room. As I began to sweep the floor, which at this point was kind of difficult because there were a lot of inmates waiting, an inmate approached me and said: "I need to pull your coattail about something." At this point, I was just as confused as you. Pull my coat tail? I have to admit the only thing I heard was tail and pull so I begin to get in defense mode and a little ticked off. I said, "Excuse me!" Later I came to find out that "Pull your coat tail." was an expression for putting you up on some news or info. I asked him what was going on and he told me to walk with him for a minute because he did not want others to hear what he had to tell me. We moved to the left side of the room and what he said next literally scared and shocked me all at the same time. He said, "I was supposed to kill you the other day."

Now please let me pause for a moment to put you up on prison life. The number one rule that we live by while being incarcerated is respect. Another thing you need to know before I go any further is that when another inmate tells you he was supposed to kill you then he is serious.

I kind of took a step to the side and looked at him to see his expression, and he had the straightest face and serious look on his face. I knew at that moment that he was telling me the truth but yet I had to keep it together and save face. I could not at that moment let him think for a minute that he had just shaken my world.

He was also affiliated but I won't get into what affiliations due to the respect for all others. This is just to bring validity to what he had just shared. So he said I was supposed to kill you this past weekend and seeing as though it was only Monday that let me know that my life was supposed to have been taken just shy of two days ago. He then went on to say that the only reason he did not go through with it was because he had been on a visit the week before and had seen my son, who was 3yrs old at the time, come running into the visiting room and jump in my arms. He said at that moment he changed his mind about taking part in the hit which brought another dose of understanding. A well-known drug dealer on the streets had put out a hit for $10,000 on a person with keloids at the prison. At the time I had a keloid on my right ear because of the extensive beating incident that I had previously undergone in my best friends basement. He wanted to make me aware that it was because on that visit he saw my 3-year-old son run to me that his heart changed. He did make me aware that others were going to go along with the hit because let's be honest we are talking about $10,000 dollars and money to a prisoner is everything. At that moment I am sure that someone is going to carry this order to kill the man with the keloid on his ear and that's me. He told me to be careful and to be sure to tell all of my people. Now, this may come as a bit of a shock to some of you, but I had my trust in the Lord yes but this news here scared the hell back into me for a lack of better words. After that, I quickly returned to my makeshift mop closet where I began to let all sorts of thoughts and reactions go through my mind. I then went to the healthcare staff and had asked if I could leave early in which they said sure. They asked me if everything was ok and I replied yes but honestly, no everything was not alright. I had just received the most shocking news I could have ever imagine, on this typical Monday, from a well-known affiliated member. No, everything was not okay but of course, I did not tell them that.

My walk back to my cell block was very different than usual because I was paranoid the whole time. I kept looking at every inmate as if they could be the one that was going to carry out this so-called man with the keloid Hit. I made it back to my cell and as soon as I got in the door I had lost it. I could not keep it together any longer and I fell to my knees and began to pray and cry out to the Lord in fear, not Faith, but fear. I was sobbing and asking the Lord why? What is this for? I had already done a very quick worldly overview of my past street dealings to see who would want to put out a Hit on me and for what. I went over and over in my mind, had anyone owed me something from the past that they felt would put them in danger if they could not repay? Did I have any enemies that I had not known? All sorts of things were going on in my mind and I was trying to ask the Lord "What do I do?" You, as the reader, should get the picture by now. I was a terrible wreck and had no idea of what to do next. Now mind you there was a whole lot of street stuff going through my mind during all of this. You see, I had been living the Life of Faith for some time by this point so there was a great deal of battling going on in my mind. I wanted to say that word, you know what I mean? I wanted to call my street peeps. When your back seems to be against the wall we all know how to get un-stuck. The only problem was that I was not about that street life no more which made it even that much more the harder to rationalize what I had just heard. In the midst of my crying out and seeking guidance from the Lord asking him "What shall I do? You heard this threat." The Lord prompted something in my Spirit. He said unto me "You are to tell no one." Upon hearing this I thought now wait a minute Lord, I cannot be hearing you correctly. I am to tell no one Lord? Not even the friends that I have here? Not even the men that I know would stand by my side through anything? Lord, you are asking me to do a hard thing. I am scared, Lord. He then replied, "I know." Lord this is going to be very hard for me to do. He then replied, "Hard for you but not for me."

Over the course of some hours, I wrestled with what I had heard from this inmate and then what I had heard from the Lord. After telling me not to tell anyone the Lord begun to put glimpses of the horrible basement ordeal before me. It was as if he was reminding me that he was with me then and that he was with me now. "Cast this care upon me. No matter how heavy it may feel trust me before you trust your men!" he said. At that moment the Lord had empowered me with the word and I knew that if he was with me then who could be against me? In other words, he was telling me this was going to take me walking by Faith instead of by Sight. I will admit, it was tremendously hard for me to go on for the next few days. It felt like months. I mean what would you do if you had just been informed by a so-called affiliated inmate that he was supposed to kill you due to a Hit being put out on you from the street. All the while I had just been given the word from the Lord to remain silent and tell no one.

A scenario like the one I found myself here gives a whole new understanding of the phrase "Be still and know that I am God". Honestly, my natural flesh side wanted to tell all my friends that seemed to live in the weight pit. While in prison that is all some of us had to do all day was hit the weight pit. I was so tempted to let them know because those boys were swollen. Then again, I would have been putting my trust in man and their strength.

Flash forward a few days and it seemed to be a typical Wednesday or so I thought. I had gotten up with the same cautiousness like all the days before after receiving the alleged Hit news. I went to my work detail with my eyes constantly looking around. I won't lie, it was almost as if I was in a state of paranoia. As I began to walk into the Healthcare door just like I would on any other given day, I noticed that something was different. The morning staff of Doctors and Nurses were running around everywhere and it all caught me off guard. I could tell something was very wrong because they were all running around in such a panic. It quickly became evident what was going on when one of the nurses ran up to me, in the midst of all of the commotion, and told me to immediately go to my office. (In other words to my makeshift porter mop closet.) I could tell that they were in the middle of an emergency situation and I didn't need her to tell me again. As I headed toward my closet I noticed all of the Doctors and Nurses making a B-line for the operating room. This is where they take the inmates with the most serious injuries. As I walked past the room I had this feeling that I wanted to look in to see what all the commotion was about. Okay, yeah you got me. I was being nosy but as I looked there was a heavy set inmate laying on the table with doctors and nurses working on him. Many were trying to close up holes that had been opened in various parts of his body neck, face, stomach, and legs. It was bad, really bad. He had been stuck or in your terms stabbed multiple times but the one thing that had hit me like a ton of bricks when I looked at him was the fact that he had a huge Keloid on his ear and one on the side of his face.

As I made it to the closet that is when the feeling of revelation hit me. The inmate that was in there laying on that table, the one that the Doctors and nurses were fighting to save, is the one the original hit was put out on. To my amazement that could have or would have been me lying on that table just days earlier because of a case of mistaken identity all due to a keloid. Talk about a bittersweet moment. I had this overwhelming feeling of relief and sorrow. On the one hand, I got a sense of ease for not having to look over my shoulder anymore. I also felt sorrow because I am a Christian and to see a glimpse that horrific assault on another inmate or anyone for that matter was shocking. At the end of the day, he did not deserve this heinous assault. He was someone's son, maybe someone's dad, an uncle, a brother. What it comes down to is that no one deserves to be hurt by the hands of anyone else. There is enough violence in our society, especially in our young men. We have to try to come up with a way to stop killing and harming one another. We are just going to have to flat out stop killing and harming one another!! It is no longer time for us to say we will "Try". Now is time for us to "Do".

As I reflect on this time in my life it could have been very different. I was faced with something that I had no control over. I was faced with trusting in my Faith and walk in it or trusting in my Sight instead of calling on men for their strength. I learned so much from this one encounter. When I cannot trace Him I could trust Him. In the end, it was Him and Him alone that kept back the hand of harm. It just as easily could have been me dying on the table that day. Who knows? All I know is that he requested that I tell no one at the time. Looking back, had I told someone it could have went a lot different. It was a simple case of mistaken identity and of not having the full understanding. I had later found out the inmate that was on the table that day was the intended target the hit was ordered on. The information was relayed wrong to the first group. They had received that he was on his way and that he was to be identified by Keloids on the skin. The part they missed was that he was on his way. They saw me there with a keloid and from there they were about to carry out orders. I am so thankful for the life lesson that I call "The Day a Visit from my 3-year-old Son Gave Me Life" How ironic; I gave life to my son who in turn, not knowing that one day a visit from him would bring life to me.

FINAL CHAPTER:

"THE DAY ONE TOUCH CHANGED MY LIFE"

Now we have come to the point in my book where I choose to share a story with you about a prison that I was locked away in at a very young age. This event was a life-altering change that I am about to share in hopes that it may help others who may have found themselves, at one time or another, locked in the same prison.

I can say to you now that it took me a very long time to even begin to talk about "The Day That One Touch

Changed My Life". It took all of my childhood, adolescent years, and most of my adult life to share these words.

I can remember so clearly how my brothers, sisters and I would play at our Grandparents house. It was the delight of our time childhood, spending time at our Grandparents house but then there came a time in which we had to move in with our Grandmother. Up until then, it had seemed to be fun, fun, fun, but that wasn't to last.

There were times that our cousins would come over and we would all have the time of our lives playing all the latest childhood games such as Red Light Green Light. My sister and girl cousins would be playing the Tweet-a-Leets rhyme game and all the boy cousins would be playing your basic sports games such as street football, kickball, hit the top, and kick the can. There were your usual times that we would get together with some of the neighborhood kids then play some of the fun traditional games with them as well. Games like Tag or Hide and Seek. After some time we began to learn the Manish games you know the ones that you never knew who made it up but somehow it seems like fun to do like Hidey O Getty O. I am pretty sure there are some old schoolers reading this book that know what I am talking about. I reference this in particular because this is what leads me to the very point of me sharing my story. In other words, it is really my Testimony because I know the very thing I share will come as a shock to many but to others may come as a strength that you are not alone.

You see one of the most under-discussed incidents in many children's lives is something that many of us have been taught not to talk about. Many have been told, "You better never say anything!" I mean when you're that young you're so terrified by the Boogieman in the closet or the Monster that we say is under our bed or the times sleeping with the lights on never coming to the grips of our fear of the dark. I too lived in this same childlike fear of what happened to me. As you get older you can't help but ask yourself "Why did this happen to me?" and you have to live with so many unanswered questions. In the mind of an eight-year-old little boy, how much pain and displacement has been inflicted when the sense of normalcy is replaced with violation of trust. As a result, there becomes a disengagement with others because of what someone older has done. This individual was supposed to be more responsible and someone that was to teach you things in life only in turn they have sentenced you to a child prison. A sentence that should have never been placed on a young boy or girl. That matter of which I speak is one that may cause you to feel that you are alone. It leaves you struggling with the blame for why this happened and why they did what they did. You think to yourself "How could I could have prevented this from happening?" You see there is damage that is left in the mind of the victim whether they are six, seven or eight years old. While the accused, perpetrator, violator, or the very family member who crossed the line of your trust gets to walk free. This individual inappropriately, knowingly and willingly puts his or hands on you.

"The Day A Touch Changed My Life", this chapter, is where I am about to disclose a pain from deep within my childhood; a pain that only someone who has experienced it would know. Which brings me to this cousin who was much older than me and my brothers and sister at the time. He was very much older than us in fact and would sometimes come over to my Grandparents house as well when the other cousins were there. Unlike the other cousins, however, his games were not traditional nor fun. His games, as I came to find out, did much more damage than good to the little boy in me. He was the one that should have been the one to protect us from harm. He was the one whose care we were left in and he was the one charged to watch after us when all the other adults were not around. Only instead of just watching us, he took that trust and responsibility that was given unto him to abuse and violate us. I can never know the amount of damage those inappropriate touches did. No five, six, seven, or eight years older should ever have to go through the nightmares & scars that are left our minds after such traumatic events. I am sharing this now because I know that there are so many unspoken violated children that are out there being left to sit in a mental prison that was received at a very young age. They are wondering "Who do I tell?" "Why did this happen?" There are no consequences for his actions due to the family not wanting to smear their reputation and surprisingly this is an ongoing dilemma in our families of today. With that being said, I'm glad to say that I have finally come up out of that prison.

I remember so clearly the day the Lord walked into this little boys man-made, self-inflicted, mental-bound prison.

That day He found this wounded eight-year-old boy who was wounded and locked away by the inappropriate touch of a cousin. I was thirty-eight years old when I was finally able to release myself from the hurt that had been afflicted on me. At the time it did not feel like I was the victim but the cause of what had happened. I was given a do not tell anyone threat from the accused then to be given a keep quiet gag order from the family after the cousin had been caught which led this boy to an un-design form of prison. After that, I locked himself in with all of the shame and guilt that never should have been felt by the one who had been violated. I share this with any and all if you have found yourself within any of the lines that were shared from this Final Chapter of this book. I just want you to know that you are not alone and that there are others just like you that sit with the same tears and same childhood questions of why.

With writing this and sharing this part of my life came with a struggle. "Do I say something?" You know this has been many years ago so I just leave well enough alone but by doing that I am robbing other young boys and girls of their release from their self-made prison that we mentally find ourselves in after our trust has been broken from the unwanted undeserved and inappropriate touch from a loved one. I was thirty-eight-years of age when I truly begin to feel the freedom of the shame and guilt of being touch inappropriately. I know that there are others that are in need of such freedom. Oh how the Lord has kept this eight-year-old then thirty years later this eight-year-old turned all of his anger, all of his hurt, all of his pain, all of his disappointment, all of his shame, all of the resentment, all of the hatred, all of the bitterness that he had for this cousin. This man speaking to you today spent years contemplating on how he wanted to avenge what had been done to him then one day he finally turned it over to the Lord. This Lord in whom gave at the time this thirty-eight-year-old peace and freedom.

I remember how the love of God came over me and how I was balled up on the floor weeping because the power of God had finally come into an area that I had kept secret for so long. The Lord knew that it was a testimony and that I could not tell anyone for countless years. He knew that I was angry and that this anger stemmed from those touches that were done to me at a young age. I cannot begin to tell you the countless amounts of childhood, let alone adulthood, fun that I missed out on because of those unexpressed inappropriate touches. Oh, the power of God's love that filled my heart that day and balled me up on the floor at the age of thirty-eight and began to release me from a prison I had put myself in. I cried, cried, cried on that floor as the love of God began to wash away that childhood hurt and pain and then my tears began to shift from tears of pain and sorrow to laughter as God was healing me. He erased all of the inappropriate touching and replaced them with the loving caresses of our Heavenly Father. Upon that day the Lord had said unto me "I have exchanged your tears of sorrow for tears of joys and gladness. No longer shall you sit in quietness for I have come to give you a tongue of a Testimony. Now share your story for there are so many that are in need to overcome what cause them to sits in the darkness of childhood prisons just as you did. I have come to give you a key to set them free." At that moment I began to ask Lord what key? Where is this key? He then began to say "It is in your testimony I have given you and so many others. The key is the testimony that you will share." I am then reminded that "We Overcome By the Blood of the Lamb and the Word of Our Testimony" (Revelation 12:11) In hopes that this final chapter finds someone who was in need to know that you are not alone and that light has come to your darkness. I believe there are countless people of all ages who could identify with such darkness. Some possibly in their mid-40's, 60's or maybe even in there early 20's that may have been impacted by similar unspoken inappropriate touches that may have come from someone they at one time would have never thought possible. It could be someone that they never thought would betray their trust and still has not put a voice to it because, as in my situation, not to embarrass the family reputation. What they never take into consideration is the feelings of the young boy or girl that has just been violated. What about their embarrassing nightmares of the unwanted touches or abuse that happen to them? I am so fed up with the families that handle such cases as mine. They give more thought of how embarrassing it is to have the child speak out against the abuse than about what may have been inflicted upon them by a family member. It is more damaging to allow a child to not only go through such abuse but to not be able to speak on the abuse. They never understanding that child's healing begins when they realize that they are not at fault for the misuse of trust by the person that inappropriately touched them or even may have abused them. I am in no way, shape or form ashamed of what I had to share about an unwanted, undeserving, and inappropriate touch that happened in my childhood. I refuse to be quiet any longer at the expense of a family reputation when in all actuality "There is a need for the Cloak to be pulled of Darkness and Time for the Light to Shine in and for the Silence to be Broken so that Healing Can Begin".

It has brought me deep admiration to share with you "The Untold Stories of Life After Life". May it be just as helpful as my first book "Risen, He Didn't Have to Do It But He Did It Anyway" All Glory to My Lord Savior Jesus Christ who indeed gave me the strength to do all things through Him. May I be just one testimony amongst the many testimonies of others that have taken on the voice to say "So let the Redeem of The Lord Say So Whom He Have Redeem Out of the Hand of The Enemy"!!! (Psalms 107:2)

By writing this book and more particularly this Final Chapter and me telling my untold stories was not to get the "Most Liked Book Award" nor "Bestselling Author" and not even for the point of winning a Nobel Peace Prize Award. My truly heartfelt writing as you or many others read upon the pages and gaze within the chapters were simply to share my testimony with someone who maybe going through or may have faced similar circumstances. It is intended to reach inside of the hearts of individuals and allow them to passionately feel and understand that there is "Life After The Life of Abuse" there is "Life after the Life of Childhood Trauma" there is "Life After the Life of Incarceration" there is "Life After Life after a Rough Divorce" there is "Life after Life after Going through the Loss of a Love One" There is simply "Life After Life after the Life that you and I now Physically Live" and that promise and strength to go on. Move on and live on is in The Author and Finisher Of This Word Called Life and that my young boys and girls, older gentlemen, precious ladies, mothers, fathers, sons, daughters, aunts, uncles, grandmothers, and grandfathers. That promise given life after Life is given from none other than from Jesus Christ himself.

In my book "Risen" I was in search of Him and in this book I am living in the life after I had found Him. Too many are dying and too many are lying in a grave unrenounced that there is a "Life after Life" and I choose to stop and mention to the few that would hear that there is a "Life After Life" no matter what you may have gone through there is still time to live".

Now I end. Help me help you write your story. We all have one God and He has given me a story but to Him belongs all the glory"

At times I often wonder if the older man standing next to me, when I am out in public in a store or a certain restaurant or maybe just even taking a walk, could be my dad. I find myself trying to find some resemblance in features from total stranger because of the scar of not knowing the reason of why he did not stick around. Never coming to the grips if I had been the cause.

Dad where are you? This wounded son is in need of you. Even at my age today I still await the day that I could place my eyes upon the one who played such a vital role of my existence. I write these few questions only in hopes that a dad in whom I long to see and come to know would be able to provide the answers that only he could give.

(1). Dad, do I look like you? What features do I have from you?
(2). Dad, would you have rather for me to Play Football, Baseball, or Basketball?
(3). Dad, what is your Favorite Color?
(4). Dad, was it anything that you were afraid of?

These are just a few of the unanswered question that I await my natural Dad to be able to answer one day. You know, I could live with bitterness about the fact that he should have been there. I could be amongst the many other voices to say he was and is a no good so and so but I choose not to go that route. I believe in my dad and no matter what he did or did not do in the eyes of others it still boils down at the end of the day he is still my dad. I respect him and surly forgive him for there may be various reasons and factors as to why he is not present in my life then or now but the fact remains that he is my Dad. I will not continue down the path of so many other abandoned sons or daughters who choose to let the abandonment of their father rest within them as a spring of bitterness which eventually become a river of anger and remorse. I will keep my head lifted and every now and then I will continue to take a glimpse of the man that passes me by only to see if there is a resemblance that he could be my Dad. I am a Firm Believer that maybe one day I just might find my Dad. I will never stop hoping, never stop wishing, and never stop praying that the Lord will allow this lost Son to find his birth giver; the man that was chosen by a loving Heavenly Father with the responsibility to train up this child. I can say we all fall short, and we all miss the mark many times and for that is my reason to give my Dad a second chance. I know many may not agree, and truly would not understand why or how I could want to have anything to do with him. They may say you are well off into your forties and you never had a run in the park or a fun game of catch or toss of a football with him so how could you ever want to have anything to do with him. Well for starters he is my Dad and I honor that, second how could God ever want to have anything to do with me after all of my life let downs and abandoning Him many times in my years. Simply put I forgive him. I forgive my Dad because I've learned how from my Heavenly Father that there is life after growing up without a Dad or both parents in my case. This is why I choose to insert my forever life journeys cry. Dad where are you? I want to know everything about you. I am not mad at you dad. I forgive you so if you happen to stumble upon the pages within this book Dad I Love You and even after 48 years I still want to say please come home. Your son misses you.

Mom, I just finished writing a letter to my dad. You know Mom, the one whom you chose to have a son with. Mom I really miss you. The day you went away still rests heavy upon my heart but I found comfort Mom to deal with the pain of your death. I struggle at times reminiscing on how I bought you your favorite Coconut Cake for your birthday and on how you so loved them Boston Baked Beans Candy and how you would buy cases of them. Mom, I so miss the times when you would comfort me and come to my defense when I would be teased by my other brothers and sister when they joked saying that I was adopted. Mom, I don't know how much you knew but Mom you were and still are my hero. My world no longer felt secure after you left. I felt vulnerable. I felt unloved. It was you, Mom, who would have taken a bullet for me. It was you Mom that would have leaped over buildings and no bounds for me. I am sharing this with you and the world Mom. You are my one and only life given HERO! When you died I was left with the void of living without you. It was hard at first Mom. I have to share it because I found the one whom I had been in searching for. You remember the one, Mom? The one that I told you about after that day I helped Gary paint. You finally allowed me to go on that trip to the Christian camp. Yes, Mom I finally found the man named Jesus and it was then that I could find some peace after living without you for all of these years. Hey Mom, the last thing I just wanted to let you know was that I forgive my Dad for not being there for me when I was younger. I know you had your reasons for why. Enough time has passed and enough tears have been shed that I am longer bitter and angry but instead I choose to be happy and free to learn, love and live my "LIFE AFTER LIFE".

ENCOURAGING POEMS

DON'T QUIT

When things go wrong, as they sometimes will,
When the road your trudging seems all uphill,
When the funds are low and the debts are high,
And you want to smile, but you have to sigh,
When care is pressing you down a bit
Rest if you must, but don't you quit.

- **Rev Wade Watts**

I PROMISE MYSELF

To be so strong that nothing
can disturb your peace of mind.
To talk health, happiness, and prosperity
to every person you meet.

To make all your friends feel
that there is something in them
To look at the sunny side of everything
and make your optimism come true.

To think only the best, to work only for the best,
and to expect only the best.
To be just as enthusiastic about the success of others
as you are about your own.

To forget the mistakes of the past
and press on to the greater achievements of the future.
To wear a cheerful countenance at all times
and give every living creature you meet a smile.

To give so much time to the improvement of yourself
that you have no time to criticize others.
To be too large for worry, too noble for anger, too
strong for fear,
and too happy to permit the presence of trouble.

To think well of yourself and to proclaim this fact to
the world,
not in loud words but great deeds.
To live in faith that the whole world is on your side
so long as you are true to the best that is in you.

~ **Christian D. Larson**

CHARGE THE HILL

At the base of the mountain I raise my eyes
To the climb that looms ahead.

And though I tremble at the road before
It is the path that I must tread.

My heart beats wildly and my legs feel weak
but my comfort comes in knowing
There's a power greater than all of me
So my faith just keeps on growing.

~ Kristen Feighery

Your Greatest Power Is...
Your greatest power is the power to be.
To be more loving. To be more courageous.
To be more joyous. To be more friendly.
To be more sensitive. To be more aware.
To be more forgiving.
— Wilfred A. Peterson

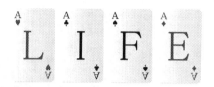

BE TRUE TO YOU

As you set out on life's road
unsure of the path you'll go,
the most important thing you can do
is to always be true to "you"

Always remember who you are
in moments of struggle or fear.
Never forget or give up on
the hopes and dreams you hold dear

MY CREED

To live as gently as I can;
To be, no matter where, a man;
To take what comes of good or ill
And cling to faith and honor still;
To do my best, and let that stand
The record of my brain and hand;
And then, should failure come to me,
Still work and hope for victory.

To have no secret place wherein
I stoop unseen to shame or sin;
To be the same when I'm alone
As when my every deed is known;
To live undaunted, unafraid
Of any step that I have made;
To be without pretense or sham
Exactly what men think I am.

To leave some simple mark behind
To keep my having lived in mind;
If enmity to aught I show,
To be an honest, generous foe,
To play my little part, nor whine
That greater honors are not mine.
This, I believe, is all I need
For my philosophy and creed.

Edgar A. Guest

Heavenly Father, I am your humble servant,
I come before you today in need of hope.
There are times when I feel weak.
I pray for hope.
I need hope for a better future.
I need hope for a better life.
I need hope for love and kindness.
Some say that the sky is at its darkest just before the light.
I pray that this is true, for all seems dark.
I need your light, Lord, in every way.
I pray to be filled with your light from head to toe.
To bask in your glory.
To know that all is right in the world,
as you have planned, and as you want it to be.
Help me to walk in your light,
and live my life in faith and glory.

OLD ENGLISH PRAYER

Take time to work, it is the price of success.
Take time to think, it is the source of power.
Take time to play, it is the secret of perpetual youth.
Take time to read, it is the foundation of wisdom.
Take time to be friendly, it is the road to happiness.
Take time to dream, it is hitching your wagon to a star.

IT COULDN'T BE DONE

Somebody said that it couldn't be done,
But he with a chuckle replied
That "maybe it couldn't," but he would be one
Who wouldn't say so till he'd tried.
So he buckled right in with the trace of a grin
On his face. If he worried he hid it.
He started to sing as he tackled the thing
That couldn't be done, and he did it.

Somebody scoffed: "Oh, you'll never do that;
At least no one ever has done it";
But he took off his coat and he took off his hat,
And the first thing we knew he'd begun it.

With a lift of his chin and a bit of a grin,
Without any doubting or quiddit,
He started to sing as he tackled the thing
That couldn't be done, and he did it.

There are thousands to tell you it cannot be done,
There are thousands to prophesy failure;
There are thousands to point out to you one by one,
The dangers that wait to assail you.
But just buckle in with a bit of a grin,
Just take off your coat and go to it;
Just start in to sing as you tackle the thing
That "cannot be done," and you'll do it.

~ **Edgar Albert Guest**

KEEPING ON

I've dreamed many dreams that never came true
I've seen them vanish at dawn
But I've realized enough of my dreams, thank god,
To make me want to dream on

I've prayed many prayers when no answer came
Though I waited patient and long
But answers have come to enough of my prayers
To make me want to keep praying on

WHAT WILL MATTER

Ready or not, some day it will all come to an end.

There will be no more sunrises, no minutes, hours or days.

All the things you collected, whether treasured or

forgotten will pass to someone else.

Your wealth, fame and temporal power will shrivel to irrelevance.

It will not matter what you owned or what you were owed.

Your grudges, resentments, frustrations and jealousies will finally disappear.

So too, your hopes, ambitions, plans and to do lists will expire.

The wins and losses that once seemed so important will fade away.

~ **Michael Josephson**

THE BLESSINGS OF A STORM

I did not know his love before,
the way I know it now.
I could not see my need for Him,
my pride would not allow.
I had it all, without a care,
the "self-sufficient lie".
My path was smooth, my sea was
still,
not a cloud was in my sky.

~ **David Massey**

OUR GIFTS ARE FOR ENCOURAGING

Help us Lord to see ourselves
Through your loving eyes,
To see what you see in us
And to come to realize

That everything that we possess
Comes directly from you,
The gifts, the talents you've placed within
Are there for us to use

WORDS OF ENCOURAGEMENT

1. You're a star student!
2. You shine!
3. You make me smile!
4. I'm so proud of you!
5. You are special!
6. You are unique!
7. I believe in you!
8. You made my day!
9. You are so helpful!
10. You brighten my day!
11. You have a great attitude!
12. Keep up the good work!
13. You're a shining star!
14. You're so talented!
15. You amaze me!

16. You are incredible!
17. You are so kind!
18. You are so thoughtful!
19. You are a joy to be around!
20. You're #1!

Printed in the United States
By Bookmasters